CONVICTION

Life Lessons From My Time Behind Bars

Shane Flemens

CONVICTION

Copyright © 2020 by Shane Flemens

ISBN: 979-8-3302-6781-1

Cover Photos by Julz Photography

Dedication

To my family and friends who have shown incredible empathy and love during my transition back to a life of freedom.

Thank you for your support and confidence as I build a life I can be proud of. I love you all.

To my mom, Carrie Brett

My sister, Rachel Ammerman

My brother, Nathan Flemens

My dad, Terry Flemens

My grandmother, Evelyn Harris

My children: Ashley, Jordan, Shania, Cameron, and Jayden.

And most importantly, to my Lord and Savior, Jesus Christ. Without His redemption, none of this would be possible.

Table of Contents

Alaska, The Last Frontier

In the summer of 2008, I was offered a fishing job on a skiff in Alaska, thanks to a Christian family I had met many years before.

Fishing is one of my passions. As a kid, growing up in Washington State, I would wake early to sneak some time in for myself, fishing on the lake before my family woke up. I would make my way back to the house in time to stow my gear and start on my chores before anyone knew I had been gone.

The job I was offered in 2008 would support my family. I have three boys: Jayden, Cameron, and Jordan; and my two daughters, Ashley and Shania. I was single and had child support obligations. Jayden, my youngest, was not happy I was leaving, but I promised it would only be for three months, a commitment that I later regretted by a multiple of nearly thirty.

If this trip to Alaska was like the ones before it, then it would likely be lucrative and was just too sweet of a deal to pass up.

On previous trips to Alaska, I had fished for king crab, just like you see on the popular TV series "Deadliest

Catch." I had worked in many of the Alaskan fisheries and even knew some of the guys on the show. I could drive the boat, fill her up with gas, and do every job on board, save function as the skipper.

"Jayden, I promise, it's only three months. Daddy is going to be back to you in no time."

The flight into Kodiak was less than comfortable. It was turbulent, visibility was poor, and the aircraft itself made noises that you wouldn't think a mode of transportation in the twenty-first century should make.

It was worth the discomfort as Alaska always delivered on its promises. The frozen tundra calls to men like me as a last frontier, a haven of outdoor activity where physical risk-taking is rewarded with surreal experiences and, in some cases, great financial compensation.

Ask the bears. Thousands of them make a home in Alaska for the same reasons we humans do; there's good fishing, free real estate under an unpolluted night sky, and the freedom to roam.

Despite this chapter of my life that so nearly could have defined it, I don't remember Alaska by my incarceration. I remember one particular hike with my friends to a waterfall where all of the salmon were spawning in the pools below. We took ice cold showers in the glacial waterfalls, swimming with the salmon and making vivid memories. Even without a photo, this moment stays deeply in my memory as the essence of Alaska.

I should have known this trip wasn't meant to be. I hadn't been in Alaska more than a few days before I made a new enemy. I was walking down the pier wearing a sweatshirt. The weather was unseasonably warm for Alaska and I was enjoying skipping out on the parka that day. However, that University of Nevada Las Vegas sweatshirt was RED.

As I made my way down the pier, a hunk of fleshy blubber leapt out of the water and thudded onto the dock between me and the shore. I was terrified. Sea lions bite people and this one seemed angry somehow. I started running at full tilt toward the boat, which was moored at the end of the planking. I didn't slow down as I flung myself into the 38-footer. But "One Eye," as I've come to call him in the years since, didn't stop either; he boarded the boat as if he owned it!

Then, it was like God spoke to me:

"It's the sweatshirt."

Like a bull to a matador, this sea lion had me pegged! The red shirt had him enraged. I threw the sweatshirt off and hid it under the table. One Eye barked, and jumped back in the harbor. When One Eye and I reunited, I can't explain it, but he had this knowing look, a sort of "I told you so" look that made me think he had somehow tried to give me a warning that I didn't belong on the boat that summer.

Dip into Kodiak

On June 13th, just weeks after my arrival and a short time into my new gig, I woke up in the Kodiak Jail. I had been asleep for two days, not because of drugs and alcohol, but as a result of the horrible circumstances I found myself in. I asked the first correctional officer (CO) I saw what I was being charged with. For the next ten minutes, which felt like some of the longest of my life, I waited for her answer:

"Two first degree attempted murder charges, first degree assault, along with second and third degree assaults."

I immediately broke down and began to cry. I cried for days. Still, to this day I cry. It would be six months before I would be able to speak to my family. They didn't want to hear from me. The COs told me I was infamous, a word I never expected to hear associated with the name Shane Flemens.

I ran with a rough crowd, I did some things that I'm not proud of, but I am not a killer. Why then did I try to kill someone? A simple Google search of my name may leave you with unanswered questions, but in short, I have been diagnosed with schizophrenia. While the court's findings indicate I was unprovoked, I challenge you to read the whole story, including between the lines, contained in Shane Flemens vs. State of Alaska. I would also plead with you that if you ever encounter someone who is in a state of mental distress or experiencing episodic paranoia, do not provoke them. Consider a compassionate response both for your safety and that of the sufferer.

I regret deeply the pain I caused to my victims and their families and learned the hard lesson that taking medication was not a sign of weakness, but actually evidence of my self-awareness. I won't detail the crime in this book, or the trial that followed, but want to provide some context for my stories and illustrate the lens through which I experienced the prison system— not as that of a convict, but that of a man who was rightfully convicted by the law, but more importantly, convicted by Jesus Christ, my Lord.

A few weeks after being taken into custody, I went in front of one of the only two judges in Kodiak. He told me I was looking at more than 220 years. He set my bail at $100,000 cash with a third party custodian, which meant that I could not bail myself out, but would be at the mercy of a willing bail bond agency to assume liability if I were to be released. I couldn't afford that kind of loan, so I would have to endure alone the long wait to trial. I didn't trust anyone and I was terrified. I was sent to the most notorious maximum-security prison in the State of Alaska, Spring Creek Correctional Center, in Seward.

You don't want to spend a minute, much less a night, in the kind of cells I've seen. You definitely don't want to live with the people I've lived with. I've cohabited with and even exchanged holiday greetings with a stone- cold murderer. I assure you; I've lived with the worst.

"Sleeping with one eye open" means more to me than a phrase from an old western flick. For years, I endured sleepless and restless nights, knowing that I wasn't in the company of conscionable, much less sane, inmates.

Un-fresh beginnings

In Kodiak I was put into one of three single cells, six by eight feet small, no windows, away from the rest of the prisoners, and socially isolated for 24 hours a day. I didn't have access to TV or even a radio.

All I got was a Bible, which I never asked for—and had no intention of reading at that point—and the letters from my family and friends wondering what had happened. Some were in disbelief. People who knew me well knew I could get into some trouble, but the charges, which had been widely published, seemed out of character. The letters told me that the media said my crime was unprovoked, and irrational, that I did this for no reason.

I assure you, there are two sides to every story.

And if you knew me, you would think the charges simply could not be accurate. The letters from my friends, despite their good intentions, were demoralizing. I began to question my own sanity, my role in the whole ordeal, and my new role in this world which I had created for myself.

When I could leave my cell for a shower— and I mean *when* (sometimes it would take a week), I would put my hands through the icy bars to have a pair of equally icy handcuffs secured around my wrists before being escorted to and from the shower by correctional officers, as if I was on death row.

Three times each day, I would position myself on the edge of my bed to grab a food tray from the slot in the door. I used my knees as a TV tray to hold up my food. I would turn my legs toward the center of the room so my knees would not hit the bars, because my cell was so small. For a healthy guy used to visiting the pantry or refrigerator at will, the three small, bland meals depressingly became the cadence of my life.

Wake, wait for meal, ponder the meaning of life, misery, wait for lunch. Nap, squint as I awoke to the fluorescent lights (on 24 hours each day), and begin the longer, seemingly marathon stretch to dinner. Three hots and a cot, but the aloneness ever-present, made my punishment more achy than acute.

When I needed a drink of water, I called a correctional officer to come and fill up my pitcher. Sometimes I waited hours before a CO was available (or chose to make himself available). I would place the plastic pitcher against the bars, and he would dump water from his pitcher to mine. The water would run through the old rusted bars, making a mess every time, and giving my water that hard flavor of minerals.

The floor in my tiny cell was wet, and I had nothing to mop it up, save for my thin prison blanket, which I couldn't risk getting mildewed. Many nights I would go to bed thirsty.

When I had to go to the bathroom— and believe me, I would fight the urge —I would ask the CO to flush the toilet when I was done. The CO, who undoubtedly had different priorities than I, might not get around to flushing the toilet for a half hour or so. The smell from the shallow, underwatered bowl was so rancid, and so humiliating. Sometimes when they got around to flushing the toilet, it would get stuck, so they say, and it would continuously run so loudly that I would have to plug my ears so as not to go crazy from the high-pitched scream of the plumbing that reverberated on the concrete blocks walls. The toilet was so close to my bed, I could touch it when I was just lying there.

Were they laughing? Were they doing it on purpose? Perhaps! But I am sure they would say no. There was a camera watching my cell the whole time, but the closed-circuit security system is designed to protect corrections officers and is rarely used to back up an allegation of abuse by an inmate.

I was terrified and did not trust anyone, not even my court-appointed attorney. I had no one to turn to. While I am sure that others have experienced worse, in contrast to our typical American lifestyle, the jail constituted horrible living conditions.

Scary? Yeah, for me it really was.

Unfortunately, the cells I found myself in during trial and after conviction and a seemingly endless series of transfers were worse. I still have nightmares. Little did I know, God was watching over me during this time of despair, He was sitting there alongside me in that putrid cell. I sometimes wonder if I had chosen to listen to His voice then, if I would have been so afraid, or would I have found the peace that Paul spoke of while he was in prison? God had his own plans for me and it was going to take some time for me to come around.

Anchorage

After I had been in Kodiak Jail for all my preliminary court dates, I was transferred to Anchorage Jail.

"It's about time. Thank you!"

I had hated Kodiak for all the reasons that I explained earlier. Little did I know, it was going to get about 10 times worse.

I was loaded into the state trooper car and transported to the airport. When we arrived, everyone was staring at me, probably hoping we weren't going to be on the same flight. I wanted to die. It felt like a scene out of the 1997 film Con Air, when the lead character, Cameron Poe, is being transported on the same flight as a serial killer. I didn't want this kind of notoriety. After all, I was in for attempted murder, with mitigating circumstances at worst. I am not a killer.

When I was arrested on June 11th, 2008, the call went out to the Coast Guard and it was all over the local scanners in Kodiak. This is a fishing community and most residents have scanners or satellite phones to keep track of the weather. It is critical for the people that risk their lives on the ocean to monitor emergency communications.

Many residents already knew I was being held at Kodiak Jail. In the airport parking lot, people in their trucks were gawking (well, probably just looking, but I felt like they were gawking) at me in my orange jumpsuit, waiting to see who I was.

The flight to Anchorage was only 48 minutes, but I didn't have a watch. It seemed like 15 minutes. My thoughts were racing. Through the whole process, I was always terrified of what came next. When you are incarcerated, no one does you the courtesy of letting you know how things will progress from one phase of your incarceration to the next. Maybe they didn't want to let us know anything about the transport process so we wouldn't contemplate escape.

A state trooper stood ready at the Ted Stevens Anchorage International Airport to trade inmates with the trooper who had accompanied me from Kodiak. The other guys were headed back to Kodiak for trial, while I was moving on to the pen.

Word about crime travels fast within the criminal community and all the inmates already knew who I was. They had heard one side of that fateful night out on the boat, and it wasn't my side of the story. I had crossed some people the wrong way and until they heard about the findings in the court case, I was bound to have a few enemies.

I was put into the back of the trooper's cruiser, with a dude who had a colored mohawk. If this had been high school, I would think he looked kind of pathetic, like the goth kid trying to make his way in the world. At sixteen years old, I would have pitied that guy. However, in his late twenties, this guy looked mean, like he had never grown out of his hatred and still had a vendetta against the world.

"If I didn't have handcuffs on, Flemens, I'd crush your skull."

I didn't reply. What was there to say? If he already knew who I was, how many others would?

My reception in Anchorage was all but reassuring. I was ordered to strip naked. I knew from television and rumors that this was standard operating procedure, but I had no idea how personally violating it would feel in that moment, even considering the dark circumstances and total lack of hygiene I experienced in Kodiak.

I was reissued my clothes and had to put on my old grungy sweats that smelled like fish. (Remember, I was arrested on a fishing boat in the middle of the ocean.) Once

I was dressed, the state trooper told me to turn around, so he could put a chain around my waist and handcuff me to the chain.

A medical professional of some sort started asking me one personal question after another.

"Do you think you may have or have you ever been diagnosed with HIV?"

"Do you have any metal implants in your body?"

"What is your ethnicity?"

"Are you taking any medications?"

"Do you have a chemical dependency?"

"Have you ever injected hormones or drugs?"

"Do you have any medical concerns that need to be addressed today?"

"Have you met with or been assigned a court advocate or attorney?"

"Is there anyone you know of in this facility who has threatened you, verbally or otherwise?" That one caused me to pause, but I didn't say anything.

One question after another, rapid-fire, and it was intimidating. I don't trust anyone at this point.

"Do you want to hurt yourself?"

I didn't hesitate. "No!"

She asked again, "Do you want to hurt yourself?"

I was thinking: "What the hell kind of questions are these?!" and, "Why are you asking me this stuff?"

She took my vitals and did a tuberculosis test.

I was transferred to a concrete room, smaller than the cell in Kodiak with just a toilet. To say I was scared would be an understatement. Moreover, I was forced to get all the way naked again, while under the observation of two COs, one of whom was a woman. My conservative upbringing made me feel gross. It was emasculating.

I was handed what looked to be a weird blanket with straps of Velcro. It was thick quilted fabric, like the blankets used to protect furniture in a moving truck. I'd find out later that it was a smock or "suicide blanket," and the manufacturer called it "humane."

I looked at the strange thing and how no idea how to put it on, or even if I was supposed to wear it. The COs didn't speak to me before leaving my cell, which I found odd. Shouldn't they have left me with some sort of instructions or even just letting me know when they would be back? With a loud rattling, followed by a thud, the door, which had a large wire-reinforced window, closed behind them.

I had not been issued a blanket, pillow, or mattress. All I had was this smock thing, which at this point, I presumed, I was supposed to wear.

Through the window, I could see the staff and inmates who were being released soon moving about. They could all see me, too, and I got a lot of stares. In a desperate attempt at modesty, I wrapped the smock around my waist and laid down, just out of eyesight of the window.

Most of my body was in contact with the cold, unswept, and stained concrete floor. I was barefoot. The walls were yellowed from pepper spray that had been used to subdue years of belligerent and self-destructive inmates. I noticed pubic hair on the floor and wondered how that, of all things, got there. I remember at one point asking for cleaning supplies but was denied.

"You might drink them."

My toilet was a metal one, like the kind you find in public restrooms at state parks. And soon enough I found out in the most unpleasant way that the toilet didn't even flush. Little bugs flew around and came out of the drain in the sink. They would sit on the toilet rim, the same rim I would sit on for 45 minutes, waiting for the toilet paper I had to request each time.

For two days, I slept on that nasty concrete floor, warm inside my suicide blanket, but miserable, restless, and wondering if this was some sort of test, a right-of- passage, or my permanent situation in the Anchorage facility.

After a sleepless night, and the dark thoughts that accompanied it, a slot in the door opened and I expected a tray. Instead, I was handed a Styrofoam takeout container with food.

"Can I get a utensil?" I was expecting a spork or *something*.

"No. Tear off some of the Styrofoam and use it as a spoon."

I ate the nasty food, but my stomach churned even more and I instantly regretted it.

A CO came and issued me "yellows," the scrubs reserved for felons. In any other circumstance, I would have been mortified, but in that instance, I was grateful for the "clean" clothes. I put them on, breathing in the faint smell of the unscented detergent, grateful for this little luxury, before I threw the smock into the corner of the cell, where I resented it for taking up the square footage in my already-too-small cell.

A doctor came in again and all I could think was, "here we go again."

"Hello Mr. Flemens, how are you doing today."

"Fine."

I lied. How the hell did he think I was doing!?

"Do you feel down or depressed?"

"Are you kidding? Look at what's happening to me!" He ignored my response, mumbled "yes," and checked a box on his clipboard.

"Are you hearing voices?"

"No."

"Do you want to harm yourself or anyone else?"

"No."

"Are you sleeping well at night?"

"No."

"Are you having hallucinations?"

"No."

A few hours later, I was handed a few pills. I declined, "No thanks. I'll be okay."

"If you don't take them, you'll need to keep the smock on longer."

"Fine, give me the pills then."

It seemed cruel and unusual, and in all honesty, it *was* cruel and unusual. However, giving the corrections system the benefit of the doubt, I also understand how seriously they have to take the possibility of suicide. Before the suicide blanket, I found out, inmates on suicide watch would be locked in a padded cell, with no clothing or a paper gown. It was miserable. Although I had answered no, I didn't want to hurt myself, something about my crime, my file, or the way I was carrying myself prompted the intake staff to take this extra precaution. As you know, some inmates do take their own lives.

I have seen this firsthand, and in *almost* every case, it is tragic.

Maximum Security

I was transferred over a dozen times during my incarceration. Each transfer was followed by its own readjustment period, new uncertainties, and new challenges.

I had been in the maximum-security prison in Seward, Alaska, for a couple of weeks, knew very few people, and was still trying to figure things out when I went to the gym to wait my turn for a haircut. It took two hours of unsocial waiting (I was still intimidated by this group of inmates and decided it was best to be quiet and wait for them to strike up a conversation) to make my way to the front of the line to get a haircut by the institutional barber.

I walked in the room and I saw a sink to the right, a barber's chair in the middle, a little shelf in the back left, and a metal cage with combs, hair clippers, a little brush, and two or three pairs of scissors.

"Holy shit," I thought to myself.

This was a maximum-security prison and here I was about to bear my neck to a set of clippers operated by God-knows-who. I mean, it's such a bad crowd that the clippers and scissors are usually locked up. I was intimidated and reluctant, but I'd come this far and didn't want to look like a coward declining a haircut after the long wait in line.

Bad idea. I should have found some excuse to just get out of line.

The institutional barber who was cutting hair at that time was about six feet, five inches tall and weighed over 300 pounds. At the time, I didn't know he was called "The Hammer." The Hammer had killed his wife and her two lovers with a hammer.

Over the course of my twenty-minute haircut, with the clippers uncomfortably close to my scalp and the back of my neck, he divulged his story, his conviction, and his sentence.

"I'll be here until I die so might as well find a trade. like cutting hair."

thought, "What do you expect? You're lucky you weren't in the lower 48 (what Alaskans call the continental U.S.) because you would be on death row."

I wished I had gone to the other barber.

The hammer knows I am "fresh meat." I've never been to prison before and the convicts can smell my naivety from a mile away.

He finished telling me his story and then threw down the clippers, smashing them on the linoleum floor.

He looked at me with crazy eyes and started breathing heavily.

"He's a lunatic!" I thought.

The Hammer didn't even look to see the damage he'd done to the clippers. He started beating his chest like King Kong and yelling:

"I AM NOT DONE!"

It was theatrical, and in retrospect, kind of funny, but in that moment, I was terrified. Too afraid to move, I sat there until he was done yelling, and ranting, threatening to kill the next person in his chair.

At this point, I honestly would have let him kill me, because of what I had been through. I was depressed and kind of wanted to die anyways, but it didn't keep me from being *physically* afraid of him. Natural fear in my gut superseded my depression and spiritual defeat.

"You are not the one," he said in a gruff tone, eventually unimpressed that I wasn't trembling.

I turned my head slowly to meet his eyes. I was speechless and shocked but mostly I was disgusted. He got the other pair of trimmers and finished my hair.

I was in there for another 15 minutes or so and he never said another word. Believe me, I was fine with that. An eerie tension hung in the air and I realized that this was probably the closest I would ever come to someone that evil. I never spoke with him again.

He is still there. He will be until he dies of old age or otherwise. He has no reason not to offend again. He can't be reincarcerated. It is just a matter of time until he strikes again.

Enter Alcohol and Drugs

After I had been in Seward for at least a year, I had come to terms with the reality that I was going to be there for the long haul. Now a true resident, I left the protective comfort of my social isolation to engage a group of guys to make my time a little bit easier. One irony of prison is that we end up there, oftentimes, because of a failure to keep good company. Once inside, however, "choosing good friends" is hard to practice. I wouldn't consider most of the people I associated with in prison to be "friends." They may have been acquaintances or even allies, but few crossed the line where they became my "friend."

We played cards, ran the track, worked out, and most of the men engaged in every possible illegal activity. They would buy and sell drugs, alcohol, and cigarettes, tattoo one another (Mom, don't worry I didn't get any!), played adult video games, watched porn, made and kept shanks, extorted and blackmailed other inmates, etc. The list of shenanigans is endless. Prison could be endless. It wasn't rehabilitative for most. For the majority of inmates it was an endless wait and huge waste of life. I decided after observing others wither into becoming more crooked, sad people, that I would not use or sell drugs, and I would quit smoking. I would come out a better man than I went in.

One day, a few of the guys I ran around with made an impressive five-gallon batch of "Pruno." It's one of those semi-genius prison inventions that is born of "necessity." For many of the guys, booze was a "necessity," but for most, it was a diversion— a semi-risky activity both in its making and its consumption, but it was fun. A long time ago, prisons realized that without proper vitamins prisoners would get scurvy. So as bad as the fruit was...think sloppy fruit cocktail, we had just enough to squeeze juice, which could be kept in a paper cup under someone's cot until someone else had the opportunity to melt down candy corn in the microwave for sugar. An inmate who worked in the kitchen would manage to smuggle a little bit of yeast, and three days later there you go, jailhouse brew, aka Pruno!

I saw it all over the place. I was intrigued, and kept my mouth shut, even hiding it on occasion so the guys wouldn't get busted, but I didn't drink it once. I was thinking of my mom and my family and how I could earn their trust back, how I could get myself out of prison and redeem my life.

Shank

Almost everyone in prison partied, drank, and used drugs. There were fights every day, but one day stands out in my memory as the most frightening.

I was playing Xbox in my cell (one of the few luxuries I was afforded based on my tenure and decent behavior) when Ryan came in with his necklace in one hand and holding his chest with the other. His shirt and face were wet with fresh blood. I fought back the urge to say "I told you to stop drinking, dumbass!" I expected he had either just recovered from a bloody nose or he had given one to someone else who had, in turn, bled all over his shirt. Except for the blood, he looked steady, but he then said three words that would haunt me forever:

"I got stabbed."

He pulled his hand away from his bloodied tee shirt, revealing a hole that wasn't the shape or size I had expected for the amount of blood. He lifted his shirt and, in disbelief, I observed a hole in his chest.

"What happened?!"

"For no reason, he just started attacking me, ripping off my necklace, and then he stabbed me."

I was surprised he was able to say that much, given the amount of pain he must have been in.

Ryan, the victim in this case, was one of the best fraudsters in the country. He forged checks and bankrupted people. Con man. Made millions. Wanted by the FBI. He would send inmates bath salt, a pseudonym for psychoactive designer drugs. He robbed post offices. He would borrow phones to make personal calls and by the time he returned the phone to the willing lender, he would have emptied his/her bank accounts.

Ryan's crimes were white-collar and he was less violent than most. However, in the adjacent block there was a hitman named Aaron, infamous for stabbing people, and now, thanks to our proximity, Ryan had paid a high price for living in a really rough "neighborhood."

After the stabbing and his rehabilitation, Ryan said he was done drinking and was not going to hang out with the party crew anymore. Not even a week later, he was into the same stuff. To the best of my knowledge, today he is still in Hudson Colorado Correctional Facility; likely shooting up drugs, with the FBI breathing down his neck to investigate the fraud and scandals that continued long after he was caught. Sadly, he has little respect for his kids or life. Clearly, sometimes a wake-up call just isn't enough. God save him.

The Punk

There was a guy arrested for driving while intoxicated. He had a drinking problem, and it was his fourth DWI and second felony for driving drunk that landed him in prison with the best of us. He was sentenced to four years. As a smaller-framed, less-than-hardened criminal who really couldn't look out for himself, he chose to pay rent, or "punk." That means that he paid the big guys (the ones who ran the prison) somewhere between $10,000 and $15,000 to walk the yard instead of sitting in solitary confinement. They provided him with protection. It was a racket.

During the holidays the prison would have a special sale, and inmates were allowed to buy cheeses, sausages, fish, candies, and all sorts of other treats. This year, we each were allowed to only spend a certain amount, and the punk wanted to eat his own food. Nothing wrong with wanting to eat your own food, right? Unfortunately, one of his so-called loyal friends had a different idea.

When the packages arrived, the punk's so-called friend for the last two years asked him to pay for a drug deal with his treats; a deal that the punk had nothing to do with. The punk said "no", infuriating the so-called friend who went to his locker, grabbed his MasterLock, put it in a sock, and started beating the punk over and over. My skin crawls and my stomach turns telling this story. It was a gruesome, horrible thing to watch, but like most assaults in prison, it was impossible to intervene. Finally, the sock ripped and the lock flew across the room.

The drunk driver just lay there, bleeding all over, until the COs rushed in and put everyone on lockdown until he could be evacuated.

I had a way of putting other inmates at ease and was able to talk to both parties after the assault. Both confirmed, the whole thing went down as a result of the punk saying "no" to sharing his holiday goodies.

Both the so-called friend and the punk went to the hole. Once staff found out what happened, they released the punk. Unfortunately, the damage was irreparable: one side of his face was beat in and his cheek bone displaced. Money could only buy him so much safety. He was covered in dark, solid bruises, like the kind you see on an elderly person when they fall and bruise like a peach. Cuts and stitches stood out on his forehead, and the skin above and below both of his eyes was solid black.

All because he wanted to eat his own food and said "no" to the deal. Please stop whatever it is you are doing that has you on the path to prison! You can say no now to bad choices and friends. However, once inside prison your "no" will be worthless. Your consent is neither requested nor required, and there is a chance you won't make it out alive. The so-called friend with the lock in the sock was a murderer, serving a life sentence, and had nothing to lose. Like the Hammer, he will strike again.

Lasting Effects

Years later, the DWI, once-punk guy was sent to Kenai, where we reconnected as I helped him get his GED. He was scarred physically and mentally. One of his eyes was permanently damaged by the chunk of metal he was beaten with in that dirty prison sock. He was still afraid, living each moment as if he might be assaulted again. He feared people, ironically even the people who would help him heal from his post-traumatic stress. His medications, prescribed to quell his anxiety, would do that and more as he battled the side effects and the prison quacks who chose dosages as arbitrarily as the scratch-off lottery tickets they bought on the way home.

I stuck up for him to a certain extent, so long as he stayed the course (which, for the most part, he did), while studying for his GED.

It was scary. Not just for him, but for me too. After all, I could have easily been the victim, and he could easily have been the witness. Years have passed, and I still look over my shoulder every day.

If Only He Would Have Said "NO"

My cellmate, John, was a murderer.

It was 10:00 p.m. on August 6th, two hours before John's birthday 23 years ago. A friend showed up at John's apartment wanting John to drink with him. John didn't drink, so he said no. He had just split up with his girlfriend a couple of weeks before. He was missing his newborn son and was depressed.

"Come on, man! You can't stay here all night crying. Get in the car."

John reluctantly agreed and hopped in, riding shotgun. They stopped to pick up another friend, James. James strolled up to the Honda, sloppily transferring a bottle of whiskey to his left hand so he could open the rear door.

"Yo, John. Long time, no see. I heard you have a rugrat now. Congratulations. Cheers."

He offered the bottle to John. "Nah, I'm good." John glanced at the clock. It was midnight. He was 21. This was not the life he had imagined.

"I fucking hate my life right now. That bitch won't even let me see my kid."

He looked down. The streetlights were too bright. He was sober, but everything felt stronger and more intense than usual. He could smell the rain on the street. He could hear his friends breathing and it was making him angrier. The driver took a turn, not too fast, but it turned his stomach and made him look back up. The guys had started talking about something else, but John didn't know what. He interrupted:

"Can we drive past her house?"

He had a suspicion that he might see that black truck in the drive. He didn't know what he would do if the guy was there, but he just had to know—had she already moved on?

Up until this point, John would have had control. He'd kept his cool when his girlfriend walked out. He'd resisted the urge to call, the nagging temptation to follow her and threaten to take their son. Where would he have taken the baby anyway? He didn't know how to mix formula, much less raise a kid.

Finally, John choked out the words: "Where's the bottle?"

It wasn't more than an hour before all three guys were drunk.

My celly stumbled at this part of his story— he inexplicably wanted to talk to her. He tripped out of the car, and up to her door. His knock was harder than he had meant. Shit. He didn't want to scare her, but he wanted to make sure she heard him. He felt like he could hardly hear his thoughts over the volume of his own heartbeat. No one answered. John knew she was home. He couldn't stand that she wouldn't answer. He was helpless to fix his own misery and convinced his friends to drive him home, where he finished off the beer they had left at the apartment.

I was surprised at how easily I could commiserate with John. How could you not have empathy for a heartbroken 21-year-old father? I no longer saw the hardened 44-year-old killer with whom I shared a 10' x 10' cell, but was completely engrossed in his story. In this moment of vulnerability my cellmate became more human to me.

My sympathy for John didn't last too long, however. His story took a quick turn from the rational when he told me how his sadness turned to rage.

In his stupor, John managed to grab his .357 Magnum from the closet, and made his way back to his ex's house, on foot. His friends, who had been trying to convince him to come back to James' house, tried to stop him, but John was so enraged that he yanked the revolver from the pocket of his hoodie and started shooting at his friends, missing them by inches.

Without stopping to consider the consequences of what he had just done, he continued to his ex-girlfriend's house and started banging on the door. Again, no answer. John walked around back, broke the kitchen window, ignoring the shards of glass that protruded from the window frame, crawled through, and went to the bedroom, where the woman he loved and her new boyfriend were in bed.

Here, his actions separated him from a rational, moral person.

John decided he would kill her.

John smashed the handle of the gun into the man's face. They argued, and my celly shot the boyfriend in the head.

"Stop! John, stop!" his ex shrieked.

John, tears streaming down his face, choked out:

"Why did you do this to me?" before pulling the trigger a second time, committing his second homicide in a matter of seconds.

John was relating the details of his story to me in a matter-of-fact way. He wanted to launch into the narrative of how he was taken into custody, his legal proceedings, and how he came to be at this prison, but I had to ask:

"Why did you do it, man? It doesn't make sense. I thought you wanted her back. Damn, your kid was *in the house*!"

Even after all the time he had been in prison, my cellmate's logic hadn't improved. He looked at me soberly and said, "I just didn't want my son to grow up without me."

Well, John's son is 23 years old now and has never met his father.

For most of his sentence before moving into my cell, John lived in the protective custody (PC) mod. He didn't participate in programs or any of the activities that made prison life tolerable or productive because he was afraid of the other inmates. Domestic violence offenders don't fare well in prison. Even hardened criminals can sometimes empathize with families and victims, and they don't take kindly to men who beat or kill their wives and children.

All day long John sits in our cell, and watches other inmates do what they do. Every day he wishes he had said no to that first drink, to his own emotions which he let drive his life to the temptation to take that gun from the closet, and to the evil that drove him to kill not only those two victims, but destroyed his own life, and left his son orphaned.

I'm writing this to get through to you, so that when the time comes you can say no to drugs and alcohol. There is truth in the proverb: "Wine is a mocker and beer a brawler; whoever is led astray by them is not wise." Pray for wisdom.

Merry Christmas

Not everything about prison was so God-forsaken. There were moments of redemption peppered throughout the corrections system and an individual's time within it. The rare authentic friendship, spiritual conversion or realization, or even a successful social interaction gave inmates hope, while the next act of violence could send us all reeling back into a state of depression, fear, or anxiety.

Holidays could have either effect. I'll admit that my first Thanksgiving and Christmas behind bars were marked more by feelings of loss than of warmth and fellowship. But by my third year, as prison took on a slight feeling of hominess or familiarity for me, the spirit of the season started to permeate the walls. And I noticed a tangible change in the spirits of other prisoners as each day of our sentences was checked off and we inched a day closer to Christmas. In 2011, many of us would crawl out, however briefly, from a state of self-loathing to orchestrate a wonderful Christmas fundraiser for the less fortunate children of Kenai, Alaska.

On December 2nd, the Salvation Army came to Wildwood Correctional Center in Kenai with an arsenal of toys and an army of volunteers. They brought Christmas gifts for the inmates and COs to give to our children. We were humbled to know that despite what society may have thought of those of us on the inside of the fence, there were still people who not only wanted to support our children, but wanted to support *us, the inmates,* in our efforts to support our children. They didn't bring the donated toys directly to our children's homes; they brought the gifts to *us* so we could share in the process of giving gifts to the kids.

On the way over to the gym, which we had done our best to decorate for the holidays, a CO fell into step alongside me and remarked:

"This is absolutely wonderful what they are doing for us and our kids. We should do something to say thanks."

I pondered on that for a couple days before the good Lord gave me an idea for a fundraiser.

I started to track down the often-rigid superintendent, Mrs. McCloud, and when I found her walking through the prison, I told her what I wanted to do.

She was a stickler, but she was usually out and about talking to inmates, which made her more approachable than most. I had some business know-how and knew I could make the fundraiser work practically, but I wanted her feedback, and, hopefully, her permission.

She told me to give her a proposal on how, when, and where the fundraiser would take place. I scrambled. Putting together a proposal wasn't something I was used to doing, and this was the first time in a long time that I felt an entrepreneurial spirit. Three days later I went to her office with a few inmate "colleagues" and handed her the proposal. I pitched it, and it was a perfect strike.

"Okay, Flemens," she said, surprising me a bit, "It's a great idea. I don't think the prison has done anything like this in its history. You have your work cut out for you."

I was extremely nervous about how the other inmates were going to respond, because I was letting God lead, and I was putting my heart into it. Guys made anywhere from $0.25 to $0.50 per hour depending on their prison jobs. It's not like they could make a discreet donation from their drug money, which was largely being banked outside the prison system, so the money would have to come from their Offender Trust Accounts (OTAs), which were much less prosperous.

I put up flyers on all four floors of the Wildwood Jail and made a banner for the fundraiser. I lived on the first floor, and I went to every room asking inmates to help the children. One after another, inmates started writing checks from their OTAs. Donations ranged from $0.50 all the way to $101.00. Inmates all over the jail would ask me for updates. I was the walking donation "thermometer," except that with humble expectations we hadn't event set a goal. When I would tell the other guys how much money we had raised, they were inspired and motivated. Some asked for their checks back so they could increase their donations!

I could not believe what was going on; everyone was filled with love and compassion. We couldn't agree on much, but everyone seemed to have a soft spot for the kids. Even though the charitable vibe only lasted for a couple days, it sure was nice. While the fundraiser was for the kids, it had benefits for us as well. For the first time since I was incarcerated, I felt people cared about what I was doing and what I had to say. For the first time other prisoners shared that they felt empowered to do something positive. Making reparations from prison is difficult and many of us felt stuck in the sense that we could not repair our relationships or our communities from behind bars. The gesture of organizing a charitable event or contributing financially to the community was therapeutic.

On December 14th, I went to Mrs. McCloud and handed her all the checks and told her how much money we had raised.

"You're kidding. No way, Flemens! Are you serious?"

"Yes, ma'am. It's over $1,000 in honest money."

"Well, I'll let you know if all of the checks clear."

$1,000 is 2,000 hours of labor collectively donated. It's a year's wage.

A few days later, after everything had cleared, Mrs. McCloud hand-delivered $1,000 dollars to the Salvation Army for the little children of Kenai, a coastal town southwest of Anchorage. I don't doubt for a minute that God had a hand in everything that happened in Kenai Jail that Christmas. Amidst the depression, despite the sin, and counter to the culture that pervaded every aspect of prison life, the Lord was powerful to change the lives of His people.

Tread Lightly

Guys in jail talk. Have you ever had a conversation where you realized that everything you had said could and would be used against you? My best example is the car salesman who asks you all about your family and how much you love your kids. He warms you up, gets you to divulge, then uses little Jimmy's name to convince you that your family really needs the $40,000 minivan with the five-star rating. Well, salesmen and convicts have a lot in common.

In prison, I came to realize that many of the personal anecdotes that were shared with me were really attempts to get me to open up and share something that would make me vulnerable to blackmail or reveal a weakness that could be exploited by other inmates, should they ever need something from me. I learned from observation, that by listening, I could keep myself entertained with stories without divulging too much about myself. On the occasion that I got the full story from another inmate, I usually gained an ally as they felt they could use me as a sounding board or, in some cases, as a counselor.

Remember the conman who the FBI really wants to talk to, the guy who was stabbed by a hitman? After a few months rooming with Ryan, he was all too eager to brag to me about his past exploits.

"Yeah, so I used to work as a car sales guy."

Oh, the irony!

"I kinda used the cars like my own personal fleet. It was awesome, man. I only put a few miles on my own baby, but I got to go out every night with a new set of wheels."

The conman explained he would leave a key out of the lockbox during the evenings, so he could come back and take any car that he wanted, taking advantage of the too-trusting dealership owner.

Ryan was not your intellectual, likable conman, like the infamous Frank Abagnale, played by Leonardo DiCaprio in the 2002 movie "Catch Me If You Can." This guy may have started out as just mischievous, but his lack of conscience eventually made him ruthless.

Well, one night, like most nights, he had had a few too many PBRs. As he was backing up one of his stolen whips, he smashed into a light pole and destroyed the backend of the car. He wasn't fazed because he had plans to start taking the cars anyways and selling them as if they were his own. Ryan went and hid the car. His boss didn't notice the car was missing until after three days, and by that time, the title had mysteriously gone missing too.

After Ryan had the title for the first car, he started some criminal side gigs to fuel his drug habit. He was hiding out in Alaska because he was wanted elsewhere for committing mail fraud. The United States Postal Service had received over 7,000 complaints of stolen mail, all linked to this guy.

One thing leads to another for those in criminal enterprise, and soon enough, Ryan decided to rob a bank. He and an acquaintance (or should I say "accomplice"?) drove up to North Pole, a cute Alaskan city with a jolly Christmas theme—an unlikely backdrop for a heist. The execution phase of the armed robbery went smoothly, as far as my limited research on the topic showed. However, sliding through the candy-cane lamppost-lined streets, a camera recorded Ryan's getaway. Days later, detectives notice the smashed fender of the getaway car caught on film, and a BOLO was issued. Every cop in Alaska was now looking for this car. In the perceived safety of their dirty motel room, Ryan and his buddy took a breather and mustered the courage to lug in the money bag from the trunk of the car.

"$4,090. Dammit, Ryan! We could have made more printing two fake IDs, or robbing a shoe store, and it would have been half as risky."

"Shut up. You agreed it would be worth it. We can call it a practice run."

The men have no idea about the BOLO, or that they needed to jettison the incriminating car.

Ryan went on a bender and spent his share in just a few days. Reeling from withdrawals, he needed more money. He considered selling his last asset (and biggest liability), the car. Being the wonderful guy that he was, Ryan decided to sell the car instead of ditching it. "Certainly, out there in the universe was a soul in need of a new set of wheels," he thought. So, Ryan set out for the Anchorage suburbs to look for someone to buy the car.

It gets worse.

Desperate for his next hit, Ryan remembers a kid that he met at the dealership, looks through his notes, and calls him up. Ryan offers the deal of a lifetime: $1,600 and the title right then and there.

"The only thing wrong with the car is the rear end, right?"

"Yeah, it's practically new. Dealer just wants to get rid of it rather than repair it. Someone took it for a test drive, backed it into something, and then we found out they didn't have insurance. $1,600, man. Take it or leave it."

The kid thought he was the luckiest kid on earth. He handed over a thick wad of cash—his entire savings from a summer spent working at the docks. They part ways with Ryan free of his albatross at last.

Out in town, a rep from the dealership recognized the missing vehicle and took note of the suspicious damage to the rear. Eventually, the kid gets a phone call from the dealership's owner.

"I know you wanted that car. We spent two hours talking about it and you said you didn't have more than two grand. Then it goes missing a few days later? Look, kid, I'm doing you a favor. You can return it right now and pay for the damages and your life won't be ruined, or I can call the cops and you'll go to jail for grand theft auto."

Some advice? Look into what you are buying, and know who you are dealing with. This kid said yes to the wrong deal. He lost all his money *and* his car. He was questioned, a process that probably rattled his nerves and made him regret ever having shopped for the car in the first place.

The police eventually arrested Ryan, the bank-robbing conman-turned-stabbing-victim, and believe me, even convicted and incarcerated, he was still the subject of several investigations.

I've only spoken to a few people like Ryan before, the kind who are seemingly born without a conscience. Some people call them psychopaths; they have zero empathy for others, and an inability to feel shame. He talks about his transgressions as if objectively telling a story. Maybe he's a victim of his chemical dependency, but most likely, I think, he's just a selfish human, who was never loved, much less raised properly. The system won't reform him. If he's ever allowed out, he will offend again, and again.

Brotherly Love

Kris was in his early 20s when I met him at Wildwood Pre-Trial Facility.

"Shane, do you play handball?"

"Nah, that's not really my thing."

"Well, what do you do with your two hours?"

At Wildwood, we were in a pod where we were locked down except for a single period of two hours each day. Using a system called "tier racking," prisoners would participate in activities like watching TV, taking a shower, using the phones, and working out in staggered groups.

"Good point. I don't really do anything."

Kris taught me how to play handball and we quickly became close friends. He was persistent in talking to the chaplain here at Wildwood to get me in the faith-based Alpha program. God bless him.

As I got to know Kris, I learned how this unlikely convict wound up in the same shithole with serial killers, rapists, and every flavor of dangerous criminal. Kris had struggled with drug addiction since he was a teenager. As is common with so many of the criminals I met, he was keeping bad company.

At only 19, he and his girlfriend, Amy, both had warrants out for their arrest related to drug charges. Kris had been arrested for possession but was fortunate to have the judge send him to Serenity House for treatment. He got kicked out of the program, however, and was told he would be meeting with his lawyer to discuss next steps (which probably meant a return to jail.) Kris bailed. He wasn't going to be taken back into custody, so he ran from Serenity House and for a few months, he and his girlfriend, Amy, had been on the run.

One night, Kris and Amy were at church, although at this point in his life, Kris wasn't interested in attending services. They were high, and they were making a drug deal in the parking lot. A state trooper spotted the suspicious exchange and as they were leaving, tried to pull them over. Stoned and somewhat clueless, Kris and Amy didn't even realize they were being pulled over. When they went southeast to Kenai and the other car from the drug deal went northwest toward Soldotna, the trooper called for backup, but pursued the other car.

Whether they were evading the police or not wasn't really relevant; they both were already wanted. Kris and Amy continued their way to their friend's cabin just a few miles up K-Bench Road, where Dustin, Kris's brother, was having a bonfire and drinks with friends.

They made it to the bottom of the cabin's driveway before the police caught up. This time, Kris had the presence of mind to stop the car.

"Sir, can you give me your name and date of birth?"

"Dustin Blank, May 7, 1986."

It was the only name Kris could think of in his panic. His heart was beating out of his chest and he thought to himself that at least his brother didn't have a record, so everything should pan out.

"Did you just come from Christ's Church just a few miles north of here?"

"Yeah, we accidentally pulled into that parking lot. GPS gave us wrong directions," Kris lied.

"And you didn't see my colleague turn his lights on as you were leaving?"

"Um, at first I thought he was trying to pull us over, but then he followed a different car, so I just left."

"And you said your name is Dustin Blank?"

"Yeah."

"Okay, well, have a nice night. Thank you for clarifying."

The officer went back to his car, and to Kris and Amy's amazement and relief, he left!

250 feet up the driveway, Dustin was sitting in the cabin, watching Kris and Amy interact with the police. When they walked in, he asked

"Hey, what was that?"

"Nothing, cop thought he saw something he didn't see," Kris lied again. "Thought we'd stop by and see if you wanted to come back to our place."

Dustin convinced them to stay. "Everyone here's pretty much past the point of driving tonight," he said. "Just relax."

Kris and Amy found their way to the middle of the cabin and cuddled up in an oversized recliner together, talking to Dustin.

"It's been a while, man. Why haven't you been home?" Dustin asked.

Kris, a little embarrassed to admit that he'd been on a bender and he and Amy were wanted, told his brother:

"I don't know. Just needed to get away from the drama with the family, you know?"

If he hadn't been selling drugs, he would have had more time to spend with family, but Kris knew his dealing put his mom at risk, and he and Amy were high most of the time, anyways. It just hadn't made sense to be at home. Plus, he couldn't stand the judgy looks he got from his extended family.

Kris wasn't in the mood to talk. He was still rattled by the encounter he'd just had with the police and didn't want to be interrogated by his brother. His phone rang. It was the girl he and Amy had just sold the meth to.

"What's wrong?" he asked.

"I think the cops are looking for you," she said.

"Why would you think that?"

"Well, they asked me if I knew the man in the other car, and I gave them your name."

"What the fuck?!" Kris hung up and glanced at the closed-circuit security camera display that hung by the front door. Four cruisers sped up the driveway and blocked not only the paved road, but also any route that his Jeep could have taken off the road. A few troopers were already getting out of the cars, with their weapons drawn.

There was some yelling back and forth, but Kris and Amy eventually were taken into custody, in front of everyone at the cabin, including Dustin.

Dustin, saddened that his brother was back in trouble, but not at all surprised, followed the police outside and called after them,

"I love you, Kris."

The red, white, and blue lights were blinding. Kris was furious. Why had that bitch given his real name to the police? Didn't she realize she was jeopardizing her own supply? His high was beginning to wear off, and with it, his patience and sanity.

"Fuck you, Dustin. You've never cared before."

Kris was released from prison just a few months after I met him. He was one of the success stories—the rare case where prison changes someone for the better. Incarceration will turn a person one of many ways. There's no exact recipe for how someone will turn out after marinating in the corrections system for days, weeks, months, or years. I sincerely believe God had everything to do with Kris's path and his earthly redemption.

"I'm going to live with the Smiths!", Kris exclaimed one evening across the table in the cafeteria.

I was surprised, but at the same time, somewhat relieved. Kris's future was all but assured.

When Kris was released, a Christian family he met through the Alpha program asked him to live with them. They ultimately supported him in a life that otherwise wouldn't have been possible. The Smiths had a special conviction that their God-given ministry was very valuable to the prison population.   They helped inmates find work—sometimes a real challenge given the convict's backgrounds, and in some circumstances, even gave them a sober place to live, amongst their own family. It sounded like Kris had hit the jackpot. I wish that was the end of the story.

Adversity and tragedy seem to haunt so many of the men I met in prison.

It was only a few weeks before Kris's scheduled release when he placed a call that would devastate him and send him reeling back into depression.

Around noon, a corrections officer came to our cell. "Blank, get dressed and follow me." There was never a "please" or "thank you" with the COs unless they were new and still intimidated by the inmates. Usually they barked orders, as if we were in basic training.

Kris groaned and reluctantly started to put his arms through his orange scrub shirt. He followed her out of our cell, down the grated metal staircase, toward the booking office. She directed him toward a little room he hadn't seen before, with a table and a grimy, corded phone.

"When it rings, pick up." She left the room.

To this day, Kris hates the sound of old-fashioned phones. When he picked up, he recognized his mother's voice. She was hysterical.

"Hi momma. You okay?"

"Kris, sit down. I just can't even breathe, baby. I have to tell you something."

She paused. Kris waited with bated breath.

"Your brother, Dustin. He's dead. They shot him."

At this point, she didn't know who had really shot Dustin, but she knew that her eldest son was dead.

The words sent shockwaves through Kris's system as he leaned forward and physically started to heave. His vision blurred and he choked out:

"What happened?"

"I don't know. I think the cops shot him."

His mom had received a call from the state prosecutor only a few days before, but had been unable to reach Kris, adding to her distress. Kris's brother had been murdered—in cold blood.

Kris was enraged. He was sitting in this tiny room that was worse than a cell—maybe only five feet by five feet, and it was hot. Really hot. Kris thought it was the police, likely the same local police who arrested him in the first place who had now shot his brother. His anger gave way to devastation and he sat in the room to process. He didn't want the CO to see him until he had composed himself.

When Kris returned to our cell, he was walking so slowly, I thought he might be back on drugs. I got him to sit on the edge of the bed, where he stared vacantly across the room, as if he was studying the dirty, vandalized wall.

When he finally told me the news, I knew immediately that this wouldn't be a typical period of grief. Kris was grieving not only the loss of his brother, but his inability to make amends now, something he had hoped to do on his release.

Sharing information with prisoners wasn't a priority for the COs, so it was weeks before Kris found out that it hadn't been the police who killed Dustin; it was a local lunatic with a history of illegal firearms and drug possession. Dustin had died over a $1,300 SKS assault rifle deal that had gone badly. The lunatic had been angry that

Dustin wasn't answering his phone, so he decided to answer Dustin's discourtesy with a 12-guage blast to the head. Dustin was presumed to have died immediately.

In a sick twist, the murderer, a guy named Lance, was held without bail in a cell in the same mod with Kris and me. After a standoff with police at the local trailer park in Sterling, he had been taken into custody two weeks after killing Dustin. Those two weeks of freedom were some of the most painful of Kris' life and now Kris had to look at this guy, through Plexiglass, for another month.

Lance was charged with only second-degree murder, and would receive only seven years after stealing many more from Dustin's life and robbing Dustin's family of decades of happiness.

Many of the stories I heard in prison were tragic because sentences were issued that seemed grossly disproportionate to the damage done by the offender. In this case, the pain inflicted by Lance's lenient sentence was unjustified because there was little hope that Lance could be rehabilitated.

Dustin wasn't perfect. He did his fair share of drugs and ripping people off, but in the dope game, you don't get a fair trial. Lance had been the judge, jury, and, in this case, Dustin's executioner.

It was a cruel reminder to Kris that the world he had narrowly escaped before finding Christ was one that would continue to destroy lives.

It's because of stories like his that I desperately plead with my children, and all of God's children to avoid drugs, avoid guns, and keep company that will lift you up or push you forward, but not hold you back or drag you down.

As a Christian, I don't believe in karma, but I do believe that without God, we are often the products of our environment. Past sins, although forgiven, have earthly ramifications. Even when we experience Christ's salvation, we can be haunted by the often long-lasting effects of old associations. Chemical dependencies contribute to our temptations and insecurities cause us to go back to our comfort zones.

Kris gave me permission to share his story, despite his regrettable role, because he wanted to deter others from allowing drugs and violence to pollute their lives and those of their families. He would never be able to forgive himself for the last words he uttered as Dustin watched his arrest. What a sober Kris would have wanted to say to Dustin was "I love you." Unfortunately, there is nothing he can do now to remedy the hurt he very likely caused his brother before he was murdered.

However, there is something *you* can do now. Stop the drugs and tell everyone you are close to that you love them and want to be a part of their lives. Take it from me, you do not want to be where I was, and you do not want to be where Kris's brother is.

Aaron

Remember the lifer in Seward, Aaron, the man who beat that other guy with the lock in the sock? Well, this guy was a drug dealer his whole life and dealing drugs was all he knew. One time, in a rare moment of honest self-reflection, he admitted to me that drug dealing was actually his occupational choice and that he could have found honest work if he wasn't so lazy.

"All you have to do is put an application in, show up on time, get along with others, be a good worker, and be honest."

If he had listened to his own advice and taken even the first step, he may have found a job. But he decided to keep selling drugs—the money was good for the amount of work he had to do. Though not always in proportion to the amount of risk involved. There were always other dealers who wanted his turf, there was always the chance of pissing off another drug boss, and, of course, the ever- present threat of getting caught. But that was part of the thrill.

Aaron also wasn't above using. He didn't subscribe to the idea that dealers shouldn't partake. He was generous, liked to hook his friends up, and did not have any moral qualms about how drugs would harm his community, underage kids, his family, or friends. His girlfriend was no exception. After all, it was her choice to use, and she could be a lot more fun that way.

Aaron and Anne were enjoying a great time at a club downtown one night snorting lines of coke. As she bent her head to take another hit, Aaron saw her reflection in the mirror on the table in front of him and thought, "I am so lucky."

Anne was the most beautiful woman in the club by a long shot. Aaron had several vices: his temper, his chemical dependency, and his career choice, *but* promiscuity wasn't one of them. Aaron was devoted to Anne. She was his everything and he planned to buy her a ring as soon as he offloaded his next batch of meth.

This night didn't go as planned, however. She had been drinking at the club, adding alcohol as a dangerous ingredient to the drugs she was already doing. On the way back to his house, she started throwing up in the cab. Violently.

"Pull over, man! She had too much to drink. We're almost to my house. I'll walk with her."

Aaron helped Anne out of the car and up onto the sidewalk. The brisk autumn air would sober her up or at least help alleviate all that sweating. He'd noticed how wet she was when they were dancing.

"Aaron, he's following us."

"Who? Who's following us?"

"That guy. Oh my God, he's going to kill us," Anne started shaking and whimpering.

"He's probably that guy you ripped off." She knelt down on the sidewalk and started to cry, then gasp for air. "They're coming, Aaron."

Aaron was taken aback. She'd never expressed any concern with his dealing and he knew that her momentary panic was completely irrational. After some effort, he coaxed Anne up to the house and got her to the living room, but she refused to lay down. She was shaking and still sweaty.

Over the course of the next few hours, Aaron debated taking Anne to the hospital; she was complaining that her chest hurt and she was breathing rapidly.

"No; I don't want to go to the hospital! I was cited for possession just a month or two ago. I don't want anyone to think you've been dealing to me."

She seemed sober enough, if not for the physical discomfort, so they would just ride it out watching a movie.

Anne died that night. At Aaron's house.

Predictably, it was only a week after her memorial that Aaron started to spiral out of control. Guilt-ridden, he faced her family, who was mortified to hear that an overdose caused her death. They were hurt and embarrassed. How they hadn't known that Anne was using was a mystery to Aaron, but he figured that beautiful women somehow get a pass when it comes to these things. Her family just didn't think that was something she was capable of doing.

It became painfully apparent that Aaron, who they had just warmed up to, had been the source of what ultimately killed her. On top of his already enormous guilt he was now hated.

Remember, it only takes one time to overdose. Anne had used coke before, but neither she nor Aaron knew the potency of this particular batch of uncontrolled street drug, Anne's medical predisposition to overdose, or what the effect of alcohol might be when blended with the cocaine. Had she anticipated the pain she would cause her family, the cumulative years of depression, and the embarrassment, maybe she would have found the courage to decline Aaron's offer.

Strangely, Aaron continued to sell drugs. Although he could never forgive himself for what had happened to Anne, he failed to realize that every drug user is someone's loved one. His only concern was for his own people; no one else mattered.

"Fuck them. It's their decision," he thought.

A few years pass and Aaron finds out that his sister is using drugs. Becky. Little baby Becky. His junior by only three years. She's using drugs.

Aaron loses all control. He gets into a violent and noisy altercation with Becky and beats her ferociously, as if he is somehow protecting her by leaving her physically and mentally broken. He demands to know who is selling her the drugs.

At this point, Aaron is still selling to any willing client, even women like his sister. Yet, his rage toward *Becky's* dealer is so intense that Becky fears Aaron will kill him if he finds him. Regrettably, she does not stop using, and he finds out again and he beats her again, even worse this time.

After the second time her brother beat her, Becky is so afraid of Aaron that she stops using for a while and gets a job. She is doing well, supporting her kids, and helping her family.

During a particularly trying week with the kids and dealing with a frustrating manager at work, Becky says she is going to the store to buy a pack of cigarettes. Instead, she goes to the dope man and starts to get high again. Her brother has been waiting patiently for this day, and he has been planning on what to do to this guy.

Little does she know; her dealer's life is in her hands.

Back at home, Aaron pretends he does not know that his sister is high, but when she leaves the house, he follows her quietly. Within days, he knows where Becky is getting her drugs. Aaron goes and gets a friend and a gun and he follows her to his house one final, fateful time.

After his sister scores the drugs and leaves, without even hesitating, Aaron knocks on the door. The door opens.

"This is for selling my sister drugs."

His close-range shot penetrates the dealer's skull, killing him instantly. Aaron, the killer, didn't run; he stayed with the body and waited for the police.

"I did it." He put out his wrists and calmly let the police escort him to the station.

Aaron pleaded guilty, thus forfeiting his trial and was sentenced to 99 years without the possibility of parole.

He told me with a smile, that he would do it again without a second thought.

If you use drugs you can die. If you sell drugs you can die. It is not a question of "if"; it is a question of "when." Either the violence, overdose, prison, or gradual and painful physical decay will take your life.

A 14-year-old little girl overdosed on heroin in Alaska during my time in jail. The guy who was arrested for giving it to her will rot in prison. I promise he will have to live in isolation. He will sit, alone, 23 hours each day, for as long as he is behind the walls of the penitentiary.

The United Nations has warned that anything in excess of 22 hours a day may amount to psychological torture and the use of solitary confinement is prohibited by the Mandela Rules. The courts won't sentence him to this level of punishment. His conduct in prison might even be that of a model inmate, but his peers are already talking about killing him and the prison will have to isolate him for "his own protection."

But. This. Man. Took. The. Life. Of. A. Child.

For a $15 transaction!

And prison justice will punish him in a way that civilized society never could.

Stay away from drugs.

Routine

Seven days a week, I woke at 7 a.m. to the sound of a loudspeaker. From 7:30 until 2:00, I worked as a law librarian. Including working on weekends, I averaged around 215 hours of work each month. I took lunch from 11:15 until 12:30. Throughout my day in the library, inmates would ask for my assistance with everything from court filings and various motions related to divorce proceedings, civil lawsuits, miscellaneous grievances, and child support-related matters. And, of course, they sought help with court matters in their own cases for which they were serving time.

At 2:00 p.m. every day, there was a count. All the prisoners fell in line outside their cells to be counted, as if in a squad bay in bootcamp.

I was a GED instructor from 2:30 until 4:15 p.m. I helped inmates get their diplomas after hours or on weekends, spending 60 to 70 hours in my teaching role each month.

To mix it up a bit, and demonstrate to the parole board that I was committed to being a good citizen, I attended a class called Criminal Thinking on Mondays from 1:30 to 3:00 and Anger Management on Fridays from 2:30 until 4:00. These two classes were designed by the mental health department and were part of a 48-week offender program. It was shocking how many programs and resources were available to us, both publicly and privately initiated to help rehabilitate prisoners.

Few took advantage.

I was a graduate of and eventually the facilitator for another recovery program called White Bison. Those classes were Mondays and Wednesdays from 12:30 until 2:00 p.m. These classes helped inmates receive certificates for parole and furloughs. I took advantage of a plethora of classes such as: Healthy Living, Inside Out Dad, CAP "Criminal Attitude Program," and a citizenship reentry class.

On Wednesdays a financial advisor would visit, and teach classes, assisting individual inmates with their financial options. He helped us understand how and when to file bankruptcy. He showed us ways to improve our credit scores. He informed us how long collection agencies have to collect a bill. He detailed the pros and cons of buying new and used cars. He even showed us how to prepare different types of resumes and when to use each type.

He gave the practical advice that so many prisoners had never received from their parents, and set people on a track to remedy generational poverty.

The financial advisor also taught a public speaking course. We discussed the proper way to address unique audiences, how to establish credibility, and how to tell when and if the audience's attention had been captured, and what the signs were to move on.

Kairos

Although all the classes and programs offered by the prison imparted some knowledge, or even wisdom, it was the faith-based program called Alpha that changed my life. The program was five days a week and started at 5:30 p.m. and ended at 9:00 p.m.

On Mondays, we'd have an Alpha Community Meeting when we would pray, sing songs, give announcements and affirmations, read Daily Bread, and discuss the future and our current activities.

Then, we would go to the cafeteria where we would have mentor night. Men from the Alpha Society discussed the word of God with us and gave us hope that there were people on the outside that cared about us. The mentors gave us someone to call, someone to write letters to, someone to help us find a positive place to live, a church to attend, and even helped some of us find work. For so many of us who were alienated from our families and communities, this was a powerful light at the end of the tunnel.

On Tuesdays, we would watch Alpha DVDs with Nick Gumball. After the video, we would have a discussion on the video that lasted about an hour. Then we would again head to the cafeteria, but this time to participate in Kairos (biblically a "harvest time").

Men from the community dared entry to our maximum-security facility to minister to us, listening to our stories, and sharing testimonies of where they and we found the Lord (or when the Lord brought us to Him). It was a strange site to see in a prison—a group of fully-grown men sitting in a circle, holding hands with bowed heads. After a poorly sung worship song, we would leave this little retreat and head back to our prison life.

Anger management was a challenge for most of the inmates I knew. Whether processing traumas from their past life, or simply contending with the ugliness of confinement, many of us were pressure cookers of angst, hatred, and anxiety. Although I am sure there were secular remedies, these were issues best addressed with a spiritual methodology.

On Thursdays, a local pastor taught an anger management class. This pastor had been ministering to the prison for years, and had a church service that was aired on TV. We started and concluded the classes with prayer, our most powerful weapon against the anger that had taken root in our hearts.

The pastor taught us what we hear and see is what we think. What we think is how we act. How we act is what we do. What we do is who we are.

Trying to view my circumstances from a position of gratitude, gradually helped me shift my responses to godly ones and quell my anger.

He told us a story about a man that asked him

once, that if he kept smoking, would he go to heaven? The pastor was never condescending; he taught us

from a position of love, not authority. He shared jokes.

"Pastor, if I keep smoking, can I get into heaven?"

"I don't know about that, but I promise, you will

end up going there a lot sooner if you keep smoking."

"If I keep smoking will I go to hell?"

"I don't know, but you sure smell like you have been there."

On Fridays, we read *Wild at Heart: Discovering the Secret of a Man's Soul* by John Eldredge and watched a video about each chapter. For those who take it seriously, the book opens a door for serious spiritual growth.

Like Anger Management, chemical dependency is a challenge that is best approached from a spiritual perspective. Although I wasn't using in prison, I participated in the 12 Steps for Christians, a recovery class. This program resembles the famed twelve steps of Alcoholics Anonymous but gives the same advice in the context of a belief in Christ. We read the book as a class then used a workbook to examine our own hearts.

Saturday and Sundays looked a lot like the weekdays. I would work until 2:30 p.m. and assist other inmates as they studied for their GEDs.

I would go to the computer lab and journal the stories I had heard, such as the ones you are reading. On occasion, I went to the gym and worked out. I went to Bible studies and watched biblical movies in the chapel. I made time to do my homework for Alpha and my programming classes.

Although God was with me and I was learning to rely on Him more with each passing day, I missed my earthly family. I made time to write to my babies and the rest of my family as often as I could.

Afterword

My children didn't deserve my absence.

I have realized, at the time of my arrest, I was lost in my own world and forget how precious life was until everything was taken from me. I took what God had given me for granted. Although my crime wasn't an act of malice, my lifestyle had led me to a circumstance in which disaster couldn't be avoided.

All the things I do today are what I should have been doing when I was living my life of sin.

My incarceration could have been a tragedy and the end of my story, but God used it to transform me and convict (pun intended) me towards a better life.

The recipe for a better life is simple:

Love your brother and sister. Listen to your parents. (I really wish I had listened.) Cherish life and influence others to the right path. If you are blessed to be on the right track, help one another avoid calamity.

Remember One Eye, that turd of a sea lion? I've been back, and he's still there. Life went on and so did he. We've had our chats and shared some stories. He listens without judgement.

About the Author

Shane Flemens lives in Wenatchee, Washington, where he is the owner of ABE Landscaping and Maintenance, a successful landscaping and general contracting company and owns and operates Rise n' Ride Rentals, a watersport company with his daughter, Ashley.

He is passionate about transforming yards into beautiful retreats where people can spend their most valuable asset—time, with their families and friends.

Shane has three grandchildren, Lilly, Amaya, and Mateo, who are the light of his world.

Shane fishing on the Kenai River after being released from prison in 2015.